THE
CONCISE

Adair on Teambuilding and Motivation

Edited by Neil Thomas

THOROgOOD

Published by Thorogood Publishing Ltd
10-12 Rivington Street
London EC2A 3DU

Telephone: 020 7749 4748
Fax: 020 7729 6110
Email: info@thorogood.ws
Web: www.thorogood.ws

© John Adair 2004

A CIP catalogue record for this book is available from the British Library.

ISBN 1 85418 268 4

Designed and typeset by Driftdesign.

Printed in India by Replika Press.

The author and editor

John Adair

John Adair is internationally acknowledged as having had a significant influence on management and leadership development in both the business and military spheres. He has seen military service, lectured at Sandhurst, worked extensively as a consultant, held professorships in Leadership Studies and authored well received management and leadership books. (www.johnadair.co.uk)

Neil Thomas

Neil Thomas is the Managing Director of Falconbury Ltd a joint venture business with T & F Informa. He has been involved in publishing and seminar/training for over twenty-five years.

Neil Thomas gratefully acknowledges the assistance of Angela Spall, Editorial Manager of Thorogood, in the preparation of this book.

Contents

Introduction

A team is:

'a group in which the individuals have a common aim and in which the jobs and skills of each member fit in with those of others.'

BERNARD BABINGTON SMITH, TRAINING IN SMALL GROUPS

It is well-known that teambuilding and motivational skills are of crucial importance in business and the leadership role in particular. Managers and leaders must be effective team builders and motivators to be able to achieve their business aims and get the best out of people. The skills needed in both these areas should be practiced and improved upon on a constant basis to ensure they help build and maintain effective and efficient teams.

PART ONE

TEAMBUILDING

Teambuilding

The first part of this book aims to give you the knowledge and tools to choose, build, maintain and lead teams at work. A team is a group of people who share a common aim and in which the skills of each individual complements those of the others to be able to achieve that common task.

Characteristics of a team:

- A team has a definable membership which is sometimes given a name.

- The members consider themselves a group, they have a conscious identification with each other.

- There is a shared sense of purpose within a team to achieve the common task.

- The members rely on one another to be able to complete the common task.

- The members communicate, influence and interact with one another in the process of working towards the common task.

- A team acts in unity, almost like a single organism.

To work together effectively a team needs to have:

- A defined membership
- A common goal
- A good interaction amongst its members
- A dependence on each other to link the individuals together.

A team can provide companionship, comfort and support to its members. Teams share similar values, attitudes, beliefs, opinions, goals and ideals.

We can distinguish between two types of groups:

- **Primary groups** are small teams of individuals who work closely together on a constant basis.
- **Secondary groups** are teams of larger numbers where members do not necessarily know each other or work together closely.

Organisations are classed as secondary groups.

Understanding teams and their structures

As a leader you must have a clear understanding of team properties:

- Common background/history (or lack of it)
- Participation amongst team members
- Communication
- Cohesiveness
- Atmosphere
- Standards
- Structure and organisation
- Changes over time

Let's look at each of these properties in more depth.

Common background

Newly formed teams will need to devote time to getting to know each other while analysing the common task at hand and how they are likely to tackle it. Each new member of the team will have their own needs and expectations in relation to the newly formed group. A new team needs to have boundaries set for it which allow it to develop, but don't give it too much freedom otherwise it won't know where the limits are.

A more experienced group comes with its own characteristics. The history of the group will have an influence on how it works now. A sharing of previous success can bind a group together. It gives the members a background which creates a depth to the relationships within the team.

It takes a while for this type of group personality to form but if you want to build a team it is essential that you allow the member's time to find out about each other and carefully nurture them through this process.

Checklist: What sort of team are you working with?

- How long has the team been in existence?

  _____

  _____

- What was the purpose of forming this group?

  _____

  _____

- Has the purpose of the group changed since it was formed? Can you identify when and why these changes took place?

  _____

  _____

- How do the members of the team relate to each other? Do they have a personal history together or are they newly formed?

  _____

  _____

- What experiences have the group shared? How has this affected them and their working practices?

  _____

  _____

- What are the expectations of the individuals within the group?

  _____

  _____

Participation amongst team members

Teams interact in different ways depending on the situation at the time. Sometimes it may be all one way dialogue coming from the leader or another member; or it may be just a few members joining in the discussion, or it could be a multi-directional discussion with the leader and members talking interactively with each other. No one pattern is better than another although as the leader you should be aware of people that rarely contribute. They may be silent but they are still involved. You should ask yourself:

- Are they interested in the discussion?

- Is something preventing them from speaking?

- Is one member of the team talking too much and not allowing others to have their say?

If this is the case, you as the leader need to practice the skill of 'gate-keeping': politely ask the person who is taking up a lot of time to hold fire for a while and then ask the quiet member to add their contribution. You may need to be quite firm to be able to quieten down the talker but it is essential you do this. You don't know how important the information is that the group is missing out on otherwise.

Checklist: What participation patterns are you team members displaying?

- How much of the time is taken up by the leader talking?

  _____

  _____

- How much time are the members allowed to contribute their thoughts?

  _____

  _____

- Are questions addressed to the leader, to an individual member, or to the group as a whole?

  _____

  _____

- Do the quiet members seem interested and alert?

  _____

  _____

- Is it necessary for the leader to use gate-keeping skills to allow all team members to make their thoughts known?

  _____

  _____

- As the leader, are you comfortable using gate-keeping skills and can you identify when to use those skills?

  _____

  _____

Communication

How easily do team members communicate? Be aware that some more experienced members may use terminology that more junior members do not understand. Take time to explain any points that are necessary to aid a better standard of communication.

The skills of verbal communication include:

- Speaking clearly
- Keeping things simple without too much jargon
- Explaining things vividly so listeners can really visualise the material at hand
- Being prepared about the topic to be discussed
- Being natural, not putting on a show for the audience
- Being concise and not filling out your point with lots of waffle.

The art of listening rather than just hearing is very important. Really take an interest in understanding the core meaning of what is being said. Watch your body language; it can give away much about what you are thinking at the time. Posture, facial expression and gestures, such as crossing your arms or staring out of the window, can all say a lot about you.

Checklist: Are your team communicating effectively?

- Are all members of the team expressing their views adequately?

  _____

  _____

- Are members preparing thoroughly for the discussion before hand?

  _____

  _____

- As the leader, are you making sure that all technical terms and jargon is explained to the more junior members of the team?

  _____

  _____

- Are members comfortable asking for clarification if they don't understand a point?

  _____

  _____

Cohesiveness

The factors which help a team come together and create the 'we' feeling include:

- **Physical proximity**: working closely together for a period of time builds cohesiveness.

- **Similar work**: people doing similar jobs are faced with similar problems and in trying to solve these, bonds are built.

- **Homogeneity**: people tend to work better together if they are of similar age and hold similar values and attitudes.

- **Personality**: personalities don't have to be similar for people to get on, sometimes opposites attract.

- **Communication**: if communication is easy between a group it will aid cohesiveness.

- **Size**: smaller groups are much more likely to develop bonds between individuals.

A leader should always be watching out for side effects of cohesiveness, such as one member being made a scapegoat in the event of a failure. Also, if a group is very close it may be difficult for new members to join easily.

Checklist: Does your team show signs of cohesion?

- Do the team members work well together?

  _____

  _____

- Are there any individuals who don't quite 'fit in'?

  _____

  _____

- Do the team members support each other to solve problems?

  _____

  _____

- Is there a good 'team spirit'?

  _____

  _____

Atmosphere

By atmosphere we are referring to the 'social climate' of the team. It is not something you can see but you will certainly be able to feel it. A good atmosphere usually indicates good morale within the group and vice versa.

Characteristics of a good atmosphere:

- Warm
- Friendly
- Relaxed
- Informal
- Confident

Characteristics of a bad atmosphere:

- Cold
- Hostile
- Tense
- Formal
- Restrained
- Anxious
- Pressured

As a leader you can affect the atmosphere of your group, so, if you do not like what you find, take steps to change it.

Checklist: What is the atmosphere like in your team?

- Are your team members friendly, relaxed and confident in themselves?

_____

_____

- Are they confident enough to express fears and negative feelings?

_____

_____

- Do your team members show any signs of doubting their ability to achieve the common task?

_____

_____

Standards

Although teams have to adhere to an organisations rules and standards of behaviour, they also build their own codes of conduct to be followed. These rules are built over time usually with the longer-serving members having most influence in generating them. New team members are encouraged by existing members to abide by these unwritten rules, or else leave the team. As the team leader you need to decide if the pressure being used on the new members is justified in the circumstances, or not, and act to resolve the situation.

Team standards can be applied to:

- **Work**: how fast it is carried out, to what standard it is carried out and by what methods.

- **Attitudes**: the attitudes of the group are generally drawn from experiences of the past that they have shared.

- **Interpersonal behaviour**: what can be discussed and what cannot, where to go for lunch and for social occasions. Shared routines can keep conflicts to a minimum.

- **Clothes and language**: teams can build up their own vocabulary of slag words when referring to their work and nicknames are often developed for individual members.

- **Moral standards**: how much time is wasted during a working day on coffee and cigarette breaks.

Checklist: Are you aware of your teams' unwritten standards?

- Can you identify codes of practice specific to your team?

  _____

  _____

- Do any of the team members deviate from these unwritten rules?

  _____

  _____

- Are the rules understood by all the team members?

  _____

  _____

- Are there any rules which inhibit a good working practice within your team?

  _____

  _____

Structure and organisation

Teams have both formal and informal structures. Formal structures are normally set in place by the organisation, i.e. the appointment of certain positions, whereas informal structures are usually generated within the team itself. These can come from the influence, seniority and persuasiveness of the members. Structures may be flexible in relation to different tasks and the knowledge needed to achieve them.

Checklist: Are you aware of the structure of your team?

- What is the formal structure of your team?

  _____

  _____

- Is there an informal structure in place as well?

  _____

  _____

- Who controls this informal structure?

  _____

  _____

- Do all the team members accept and adhere to this structure?

  _____

  _____

- Does the structure alter depending on the task at hand?

  _____

  _____

Changes over time

A team acts as a unit but don't forget it is made up of individuals who are constantly changing and growing. These changes will affect the group dynamics in respect of morale, efficiency, cohesion, levels and types of participation and structure. Groups can go through identifiable stages of development but these stages may come in leaps and bounds or in a more cyclic or spiral form.

Stages of group development:

- **Forming**: The group asks 'What is the task?' There is considerable anxiety at this stage as the team works out what is expected of them.

- **Storming**: The group asks 'Why are we being asked to do this?' and 'How are we going to do it?' Conflict may arise over these questions and the leaders' authority may be questioned as they try to regain control of the group.

- **Norming**: The group begins to co-operate with the leader and with each other as they formulate their plans and communication develops. Mutual support comes into play as group cohesion grows.

- **Performing**: Work begins on the task and progress is made towards achieving the end result. The group structures itself to its best advantage in relation to the particular task.

There is another stage called 'dorming' which a team can lapse into. This is when the team structure becomes dominated by routine and systems, the group spirit becomes comfortable and activity declines. It may happen because the team is satisfied with past achievements and subconsciously leaves the new challenges to other upcoming groups.

Team roles and team member functions

As a leader you must have a clear understanding of team roles and functions:

- The role of the leader
- Team task roles
- Group building and maintenance roles
- Individual roles

Lets look at each of these points in more depth.

The following descriptions of roles are based on the work of Kenneth D. Benne and Paul Sheats in 1948 published in 'Functional Roles of Group Members', Journal of Social Issues, Vol 4, No 2.

The role of the leader

The position of leader of a team is a most important one. Without a leader the team would have no guide or direction and would, most likely, soon become very unproductive. The main role of all leaders, therefore, is to help the team achieve its common task, to maintain the teams' unity and to ensure that individuals give their best. This applies to leaders in all working situations.

Every leader will bring their own personality to the role they fill, along with their particular knowledge and experience suited to the task to be achieved. Some roles will need certain personal qualities as well as specific knowledge and experience. It's these individual traits that allow us to be creative as leaders. Draw upon as many sources as possible to gain more knowledge about your role and how you can expand it.

All leaders also have obligations to their superiors and their colleagues on the same level as themselves. This means the leader also has the roles of subordinate and colleague. This balance of roles can be quite a challenge and can cause:

- insecurity
- a lack of confidence
- a lack of clarity
- irritation
- anxiety
- stress
- low morale
- communication difficulties

and sometimes even anger from those around you.

Some ways of counteracting these problems include:

- Learn to prioritise your commitments
- Agree with your superior to reassign or delegate some of your responsibilities
- Lower your self-expectation levels to a more acceptable standard
- Ask for clarification if you are uncertain of your obligations
- Make sure you take time out to spend with family and friends

Team task roles

Each member of a team may take on more than one role within a team and, indeed, the roles may change depending on the task in hand.

The roles found within a team include:

- **Initiator/contributor**: suggests new ideas, goals, procedures or new definitions of a problem.

- **Information seeker**: asks for clarification about tasks and tries to find information relevant to specific problems.

- **Opinion seeker**: asks for clarification of the values, rather than facts, relevant to problems.

- **Information giver**: passes facts or relevant experiences to the other members of the team.

- **Opinion giver**: states his beliefs in relation to the problem or to the suggestions being made about how to solve it.

- **Elaborator**: details suggestions, and reasons for the suggestions, to solve a problem and tries to deduce the consequences of these suggestions.

- **Co-ordinator**: clarifies the relationships between various ideas and suggestions and tries to co-ordinate the groups' activities.

- **Orienter**: defines the position of the group with respect to its goals.

- **Evaluator/critic**: looks critically at the groups achievements and goals.

- **Energiser**: stimulates the group into making a decision or a higher quality of activity.

- **Procedural technician**: performs routine tasks to keep the group moving.

- **Recorder**: writes down suggestions, decisions made and minutes of meetings.

Group building and maintenance roles

Members of a team take on various roles, often more than one, which help build team attitudes and maintain them. These roles can be carried out by either the leader or the individual team members:

- **Encourager**: radiates a warmth and sense of encouragement towards other team members' contributions.

- **Harmoniser**: attempts to reconcile any differences of opinion and reduce tension between other group members.

- **Compromiser**: offers compromise regarding his own ideas in order to maintain group harmony.

- **Gatekeeper/expediter**: encourages communication and participation between and from all team members.

- **Standard setter**: expresses and applies working standards for the group to adhere to.

- **Group observer/commentator**: keeps records of data produced by the group and feeds it back to the group so they can evaluate their procedures.

- **Follower**: takes a back-seat in group discussions and accepts the ideas of others.

Individual roles

When joining a group individuals bring with them their own set of expectations and needs. Sometimes these needs can be irrelevant to the group task and hinder its progress.

These roles include:

- **Aggressor**: attacks the group or the validity of the task at hand by expressing disproval or displaying envy towards others.

- **Blocker**: opposes and acts negatively towards new ideas.

- **Recognition seeker**: gains attention from others by boasting about personal achievements and perceived knowledge.

- **Self-confessor**: uses the group as an audience to express ideas and feelings unrelated to the task at hand.

- **Playboy**: displays nonchalance and horseplay along with a general uninterested attitude to the group and its task as a whole.

- **Dominator**: tries to manipulate the group or specific group members by using flattery, being attention seeking or interrupting others.

- **Help-seeker**: tries to get sympathy from other group members by showing insecurity, confusion or a lack of self-confidence.

- **Special interest pleader**: speaks on behalf of the public minority usually covering his own prejudices.

Benne and Sheats saw individual roles as quite negative but we will go on to look at individuals in relation to the task and the team in a much more positive way.

The individual within the team

As a leader you must have a clear understanding of the individuals who make up the team:

- commonalities between individuals
- treat people as individuals

Commonalities between individuals

Individuals are just that, individual, but there are also certain elements which are common between individuals.

As humans we share certain common needs, for example food and shelter, security and preservation. We also share the human social practice of giving and receiving, and exchanging things. Unconsciously we are aware that this exchange should be roughly equal between the parties involved. This same principle can be found within teams. The rewards of being part of a group should equal the input from the individual. If this is not the case it can lead to resentment between employees, especially if another team member is perceived as receiving more than their fair share of the rewards.

One of the attractions as an individual to work in a team is that it allows us to expand our knowledge, ability and experience. This is what we receive from the team in exchange for our hard work and dedication.

All humans have certain characteristics which are developed by the environment and inheritance. Some of these characteristics are:

- Trust
- Autonomy
- Initiative
- Integrity
- Security

The level of development will vary between individuals. It is this level of development which makes up our individual personalities. For example, we all have a sense of humour without necessarily finding the same things amusing.

Treat people as individuals

Every person is unique even though we have similarities in temperament, interests, habits, our jobs etc. Organisations that treat their members as individuals, rather than numbers, are much more likely to get the best out of them.

Individuals that are not treated as such will feel:

- Suppressed
- Cajoled
- Trapped
- Pressured
- Manipulated

They will no longer feel able to use their initiative, judgement and creativity.

When a person is recognised for his individuality it will be realised what a unique contribution he could make to the common task and the team as a whole.

The overlapping needs of task, team and individual

Teams can develop personalities of their own as they grow. One team will not be exactly the same as another but, just like individuals, groups share common needs.

The needs of a group:

- **Task:** the need to accomplish the common task or solve a problem. This is what the group is talking about and is usually seen in terms of things rather than people.

- **Team**: the need to develop and maintain good working relationships among the members. This is primarily about people and how they relate to each other.
- **Individual**: the need to fulfil their own individual needs, such as food, shelter, security, respect and self-actualisation. Individual needs should be met along with the group and task needs, not at their expense.

The interaction between these needs can be illustrated as follows:

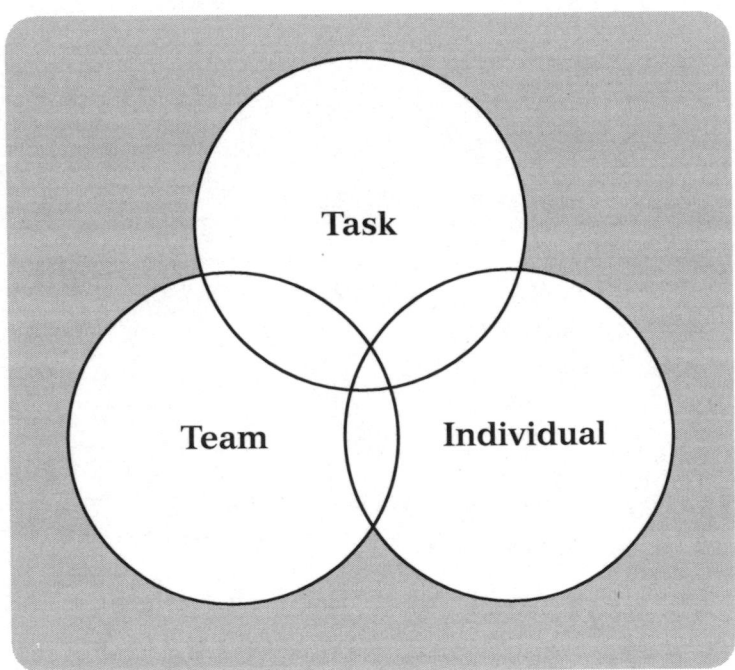

By achieving the common task a sense of unity is created within the team which will also affect the individual. A good team will mean you are more likely to achieve the common task. If the individuals are fully motivated they will have a greater input to the team and therefore the task. If one of these areas fails or under-performs it will affect the other areas dramatically.

Leadership functions and needs

In order for task and team needs to be met certain functions have to be carried out by the leader or, indeed, other team members:

- **Initiating**: getting the team motivated to begin work.

- **Regulating**: influencing the direction and the speed of the work.

- **Informing**: bringing new information to the group as it becomes available.

- **Supporting**: harmonising, relieving tensions, encouraging and motivating.

- **Evaluating**: helping the group to evaluate decisions or procedures.

If any of these functions are missing it will affect how the team performs.

Teams

It is not difficult to establish teamwork or co-operation between a group of people but it can be more difficult to establish a high-achieving, high performing team. High performance teams need a very good leader who has personal and functional qualities in both the task and team areas. A good leader will know how to inspire and motivate the team into performing at their best. This will be covered in more detail in Part two.

The other important part of a high-performing team is the team members. The most effective team members are those who can provide functions to be able to achieve the task, and who are willing to build and encourage relationships with others.

Individuals come together under a leader to form a team to try to achieve a common task between them. It may be that the task is too big for one person to carry it out in the time allocated or that several different functions need to be performed at the same time. The group becomes the instrument for achievement.

Experts in a team

Members of the team with an expert knowledge in a specific area will benefit the other team member's thorough communication and interaction. The team as a whole will become more knowledgeable and experienced.

However, it may take the group more time to decide that the expert has the correct solution than if he worked on his own. He will need to take time to explain his theories and to make the others understand. This can be quite distracting and time consuming for the expert. You should consider carefully if the task really needs a team to work on it to be able to achieve it. If it does, then the expert will need to have good interpersonal skills as well as his knowledge.

On the plus side, the group may give him enough feedback to warrant a re-evaluation of the theories and solutions put forward, or indeed, stimulate new thoughts and ideas.

Sequential teams

Not all teams work within sight or earshot of each other but they can still work together effectively. They still depend on each other to do their jobs to their best abilities to be able to achieve the common task. For example, when building a house the bricklayer builds the walls, then the joiner will build the roof, the tiler will complete the roof and then the plasterer will come in to do his work. Without each other this team would not be able to build the house.

If one of the team members doesn't do his job well it will affect the end result and let down the whole team. Who manages this type of team to ensure effective productivity? The manager cannot be there all the time so each team member has to lead himself and make sure he sticks to his own and his teams high standards. The sense of belonging and commitment to a team and wanting to do a good job within that team is what motivates the individual to achieve the high standards required.

The leader

Effective leadership comes from respect and trust, which creates real commitment from a team, not from fear or submission which produce compliance. A good leader is able to focus the efforts of the team towards the common goal, enabling them to work together as effectively as possible. A leader brings together all the parts to make a whole.

Successful leaders can be very different from each other. All leaders have strengths, knowledge, personality and character but these vary between individuals. No two leaders are exactly the same as individual personalities and traits are just that, individual.

One of the main results of good leadership is a good team:

Good leadership characteristics	Team outcomes
Enthusing	Team members are purposefully busy and have a basis to judge priorities
Practices values such as integrity	Gives a sense of excitement and achievement with people willing to take risks and higher work loads
Leads by example	Consistency in knowing the leader's values
Generates good leaders from the followers	Is trusted by the team members

Good leadership characteristics	Team outcomes
Aware of own behaviour and environment	Individuals aspire to the leader's example
Intellect to meet the job needs	Confidence in leadership
Aware of team and individual needs	The led start to lead (with leader less indispensable), being delegated to, coached and supported
Exhibits trust	Inspires confidence and performance
Represents the organisation to the team and vice versa	Confidence of contribution to aims and commitment to them

Outcomes of effective leadership

Effective leadership will enable the team members to:

- have a clear sense of direction and work hard and effectively
- have confidence in their ability to achieve specific challenging objectives
- believe in and be identified with the organisation
- hold together when the going is rough

- have respect for and trust in managers
- adapt to the changing world.

In achieving the task, building the team and developing the individual, whilst leadership **style** may differ, effective leadership (in ICI's findings and its development courses) emphasised that the leader must:

- feel personally responsible for his/her human, financial and material resources
- be active in setting direction and accepting the risks of leadership
- be able to articulate direction and objectives clearly and keep his/her people in the picture
- use the appropriate behaviour and methods to gain commitment for the achievement of specific objectives
- maintain high standards of personal performance and demand high standards of performance from others.

The leader's core responsibility

The first responsibility of the leader is to define the objective and therefore the task. Until you know what you want to achieve you cannot begin to achieve it. Once the team have understood and accepted the objective each individual needs to have their target and role defined. If possible, this should be worked out jointly between the leader and the individual concerned.

Good targets should be:

- Measurable
- Have a time limit
- Realistic

- Challenging
- Agreed.

Leadership functions in teambuilding

Effective leaders in teambuilding need to provide the functions of:

- Planning:
    - seeking all available and relevant information
    - defining the task, purpose or goal
    - devising a realistic framework for achieving the desired outcome

- Initiating:
    - clearly briefing the team on the aims and the plan of action
    - explaining why the task is necessary and the reasoning behind the plan
    - allocating tasks to team members
    - setting group standards

- Controlling:
    - maintaining the group standards as previously set
    - keeping a watch on timing and progress
    - ensuring all actions are moving towards the desired end result
    - keeping discussions relevant on on-track
    - keeping the group moving and active

- Supporting:
  - expressing recognition of individuals contributions
  - providing encouragement to the whole group as well as to individuals
  - disciplining where necessary and appropriate
  - creating a team spirit and boosting morale
  - watching and dispersing tension between team members
  - reconciling disagreements or controlling the exploration of them

- Informing:
  - clarifying the task and the plan as the project makes progress
  - sharing new information with the team and keeping them informed of developments
  - listening to the group and receiving feedback from them
  - discussing ideas and suggestions within the group

- Evaluating:
  - checking the feasibility of ideas
  - testing the consequences of new ideas and proposed solutions
  - evaluating group performance and giving feedback
  - allowing the group to evaluate themselves against the standards set

Not all these function will be needed all of the time but together they will allow the leader to:

- Build and maintain the team
- Develop the individual
- Achieve the task.

Selecting the team members

Leaders usually inherit a team rather than having the luxury of building their own but, if you are given the opportunity, how would you go about it?

Although you may be constrained by timescales or your pool of people to choose from, you should consider three key factors when interviewing people for the new team:

- Their technical or professional competence
- Their ability to work as a team member
- The presence of the desired personal attributes.

You may know the people you are interviewing quite well, or you may not, but everyone should be given a fair hearing via a process of interviewing and testing.

Technical or professional competence

The candidate should possess the relevant skills and knowledge required to be able to achieve his part in the task at hand. As a leader you may not have specialist knowledge in the required area but you will need enough insight to be able to judge your candidates abilities.

If you don't have the relevant knowledge you may need to involve a specialist who can make a better judgement. This may be someone from within the organisation or within the team as it stands.

Ability to work as a team member

Your selection process should eliminate those that are not motivated to achieve or to work in a team, or indeed as individuals. They will hinder the group's progress.

The difficulty comes when you meet people who do not seem motivated but could be, given the right environment and encouragement. They may lack motivation about their present position but could become inspired under your leadership and do great things.

Disruptive people should not feature on your team. They do not make good team members and will not advocate the harmony you are trying to achieve.

Be sensitive to the chemistry of the group and the balance of personalities within it. A variety of personalities which complement each other will draw out the best from the team.

Desired personal attributes

Desirable attributes include:

- The ability to listen to others
- Having a flexible approach to problems
- Being confident enough to express views and opinions
- The ability to give and inspire trust
- A sense of integrity

- Having professional and moral standards
- Interpersonal skills and 'likeability'.

Checklist:
Have you selected the right team?

TASK

- Does each team member have an alert intelligence?

  _____

  _____

- Does each team member have a high level of vocational skills?

  _____

  _____

- Do the skills of each team member complement the skills of the others?

  _____

  _____

- Is each team member motivated enough to want to achieve the best results possible?

  _____

  _____

- Does each team member have a good previous record of working in a team?

  _____

  _____

Continued over

TEAM

- Is each team member capable of working closely with the others in a friendly and personable way?

  _____

  _____

- Is each team member capable of really listening?

  _____

  _____

- Is each team member flexible enough to take on the different roles which may be asked of them?

  _____

  _____

- Is each team member capable of being assertive without being aggressive?

  _____

  _____

- Will each team member contribute to the team morale?

  _____

  _____

INDIVIDUAL

- Does each team member have a sense of humour?

  _____

  _____

- Is each team member capable of tolerating the views and opinions of others?

  _____

  _____

- Is each team member motivated to achieve the task within the team?

  _____

  _____

- Does each team member have a sense of responsibility to the team as a whole?

  _____

  _____

- Does each team member display signs of integrity?

  _____

  _____

Group processes and procedures

All teams have procedures and ways of working. These are usually quite informal but how they are approached can affect the atmosphere, participation and cohesiveness of the group.

Problem-solving

A problem is a task for which the person or group confronting it:

- wants or needs to find a solution
- has no readily available procedure for finding the solution
- must try to find the solution.

Therefore, the team is motivated and consciously tries to find the solution which isn't necessarily easily reached.

As the leader it is your responsibility to present the problem to the team in a sufficiently attractive way for them to be interested in and motivated by it. They should be made to feel that the solution is within their grasp even if it may take a while to discover it.

The leader needs to remember that it is the individuals who are creative and will use this attribute to solve problems. The team provides a positive environment for this to happen in. It provides atmosphere, communication, standards, morale and leadership which all contribute to the climate which stimulates, triggers, encourages and develops creative thinking.

The skills needed for effective problem solving include:

- **Analysing**: the ability to divide a problem into pieces, to dissect the whole into more manageable parts.

- **Reasoning**: the ability to think in logical steps.

- **Synthesising**: the reverse process of analysing – putting together parts to make a whole, a solution.

- **Holistic thinking**: the ability to see the whole rather than just the parts.

- **Valuing**: the ability to judge the value of something, depending on the context and conditions.

- **Intuition**: the ability to use and recognise the use of the depth mind, the subconscious.

- **Memory**: the important part of the active depth mind. It is our storage and retrieval system for knowledge and experience.

- **Creativity**: the ability to relate together more than one idea that may originally appear unconnected.

- **Imagination**: the ability to think in pictures.

- **Numeracy/literacy**: the natural ability to think in terms of numbers or words.

As a leader you should have good skills in all these areas and be able to encourage them in others.

Decision-making

How are decisions made within your team?

Group processes can work in the following ways:

- **Apathy**: nobody is sufficiently interested or concerned.

- **Plops**: there is no response to a suggested decision.

- **Self-authorised decisions**: an individual assumes the authority to make a decision.

- **Pairing**: two group members join forces to make a decision.

- **Topic-jumping**: jumping to another topic can lead to a quick or different decision.

- **Minority group**: a small group makes a decision away from the other team members.

- **Majority views**: using a voting system.

- **Does anyone disagree?**: a decision made under the pressure of not disagreeing.

Although the final decision may not be everyone's preferred decision, everyone in the team should be prepared to act as if it were. This means everyone has the same commitment to carrying it out and making it work to the best of their abilities.

When there are decisions to be made you will find some team members look to the others to tell them how they should be thinking and reacting. They are dependent on the 'authority figure'. Other team members may resist the guidance of the leader in making a decision. They may feel that the leader is taking away their freedom and telling them what to do. This is known as counter-dependency.

The dependent person can be nurtured and encouraged to be more independent and have more confidence. Counter-dependency should be tackled using your personality and knowledge, rather than blatant authority.

Ideally, all leaders would like a team of people who are inter-dependent – individuals who are free and equal and who accept that their ideas, skills, knowledge and needs compliment and benefit each other.

A framework for problem-solving and decision-making

The classic framework involves five steps:

1 Defining the objective or problem: this is mainly analytical.

2 Collecting data or reviewing the information held: this involves experience, memory, information-seeking, research skills, literacy and numeracy.

3 Generating alternative feasible solutions or courses of action: this stage mainly uses the skill of synthesis but will also involve a certain amount of valuing.

4 Selecting the right answer or best course of action: this mainly uses the skills of valuing.

5 Evaluating the decision or solution: this can be before, during or after implementing it, or at all three stages.

Brainstorming

Brainstorming is a productive way of getting ideas from a team within a short space of time. It is based on the principle of suspended judgement. When considering new ideas most people think about them critically. This can hinder creative thoughts and innovation. Also, the more thoughts that are expressed the more likely the team is to come up with a solution. What may seem like a silly idea to one person might just trigger a brilliant idea from another.

The rules for a brainstorming session:

- **Suspend judgement**: no criticism is allowed. Do not evaluate ideas at this stage, stick to thinking creatively.

- **Free-wheel**: the wider the ideas the better. It is easier to dumb down an idea than to build one up.

- **Strive for quantity**: the greater the number of ideas the greater the likelihood of finding a successful one.

- **Combine and improve**: ideas that are suggested can be picked up by others and turned into better ideas or combined with others.

Someone in the group should be nominated to record all the ideas as they are generated, preferably so the whole group can see them during the session.

After the session participants should be encouraged to voice further ideas that they have. Once all ideas are collated a group of four or five people should evaluate the suggestions. The brainstorming group should be kept informed of progress and referred to if clarification is needed.

Checklist: Group processes and procedures

- Do you make sure all members of the team fully understand the problem?

  _____

  _____

- Does each member of the team have their own way of looking at the problem?

  _____

  _____

- Can you identify the methods they are using?

  _____

  _____

- Do individuals work as a team, communicating and building on each others ideas?

  _____

  _____

- Do individuals fully explain their ideas to each other?

  _____

  _____

- Do the team members really listen to each other?

  _____

  _____

- Do the team members criticise ideas too early, before they are allowed to develop?

  _____

  _____

- Do they build on incomplete ideas or just dismiss them?

  _____

  _____

- Do they spend time exploring one idea before moving onto the next?

  _____

  _____

- Do they keep to the point or do they waste time discussing irrelevant subjects?

  _____

  _____

Maintaining your team

A team which is permanently in place can become very comfortable and committed to each other. They will have a history together which builds familiarity and a good team spirit. However, there will still be a requirement for team maintenance to uphold their level of excellence and efficiency.

From time to time it is good to ask yourself and your team:

- What is our purpose as a team?

- What and who would be affected if we didn't exist?

- Is this team the most cost effective way of achieving our purpose?

- Has our purpose changed and, if so, are we clear how it has changed?

- Are we still the right people to be doing this work?

Maintaining standards

Over a period of time a teams standards can slip. If a team has been very successful a sense of complacency can creep in. On the other hand, the team might be working to the standards it has always abided by but things may have changed outside of the team. Targets may have become higher and more may be expected from the team without them being aware of it.

Injecting a sense of competition into the teams work can raise standards. Telling a team where they stand in relation to the competitions standards should motivate them to compete and move up the ladder of success again.

Regard your team as a living entity than needs to be nurtured to maintain its growth and existence. To maintain standards you constantly need to aim for higher standards.

Coping with conflict

What do you do if there is conflict amongst the team members?

The first strategy is to depersonalise the issue so they focus on the difference of policies or ideas. Remember that as the leader you can only help as a mediator, you cannot solve the conflict for the people involved. Ultimately they have to sort it out for themselves on a personal level.

You can set them a time limit, suggesting a third party be present to help, or you could act as a consultant or change agent yourself to bring about reconciliation. As the leader you must judge if the negative emotions should be made public. This will depend on the situation at the time.

If both parties value the common task they should realise that they need to get on with each other in order to achieve it. This is usually the ultimate resolution to any conflict within a team but if the situation cannot be resolved you may need to take more drastic action.

Checklist: Do you need to spend time on team maintenance?

- Are there any symptoms of low morale, declining self-confidence or a loss of sense of purpose?

  _____

  _____

- Has the group lost its sense of direction?

  _____

  _____

- Is each team member clear about the team's core purpose?

  _____

  _____

- Does the team have a good atmosphere and spirit?

  _____

  _____

- Are individuals enthusiastic about the common task?

  _____

  _____

- Can you spot signs of mistrust between team members?

  _____

  _____

- Are there divisions or sub-groups forming within the team?

  _____

  _____

- Have team standards been declining?

  _____

  _____

- Are one or two individuals under-achieving?

  _____

  _____

- Are there any complaints about your leadership?

  _____

  _____

A checklist for team leaders

As a leader you should ask yourself the following three sets of questions to help you analyse and improve the way that your team operates:

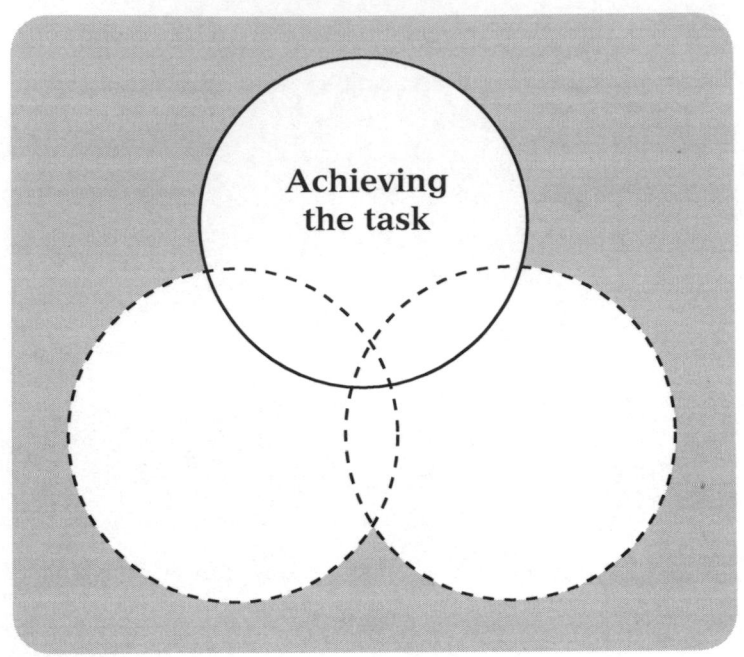

Task

Purpose: Am I clear what the task is?

Responsibilities: Am I clear what mine are?

Objectives: Have I agreed these with my superior, the person accountable for the group?

Programme: Have I worked one out to reach objectives?

Working conditions: Are these right for the job?

Resources: Are these adequate (authority, money, materials)?

Targets: Has each member clearly defined and agreed them?

Authority: Is the line of authority clear (accountability chart)?

Training: Are there any gaps in the specialist skills or abilities of individuals in the group required for the task?

Priorities: Have I planned the time?

Progress: Do I check this regularly and evaluate?

Supervision: In case of my absence who covers for me?

Example: Do I set standards by my behaviour?

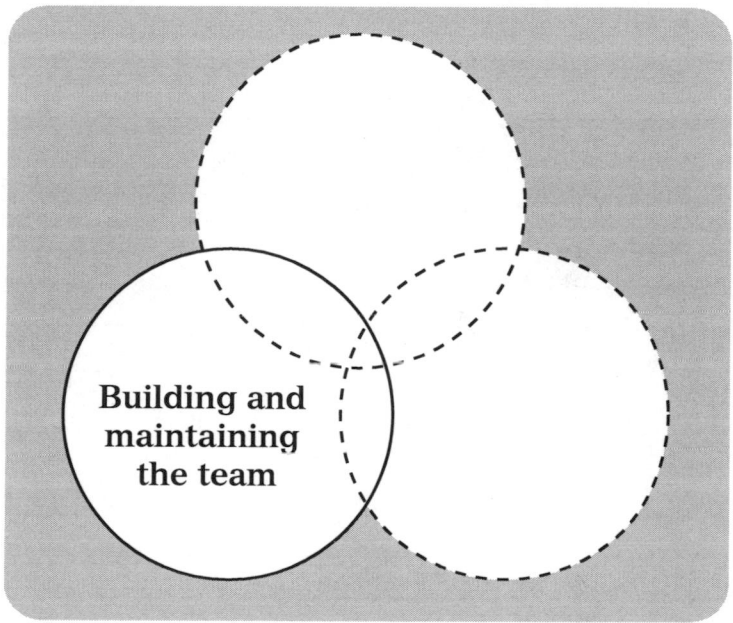

Team

Objectives: Does the team clearly understand and accept them?

Standards: Do they know what standards of performance are expected?

Safety standards: Do they know consequences of infringement?

Size of team: Is the size correct?

Team members: Are the right people working together? Is there a need for sub-groups to be constituted?

Team spirit: Do I look for opportunities for building teamwork into jobs? Do methods of pay and bonus help to develop team spirit?

Discipline: Are the rules seen to be reasonable? Am I fair and impartial in enforcing them?

Grievances: Are grievances dealt with promptly? Do I take action on matters likely to disrupt the group?

Consultation: Is this genuine? Do I encourage and welcome ideas and suggestions?

Briefing: Is this regular? Does it cover current plans, progress and future developments?

Represent: Am I prepared to represent the feelings of the group when required?

Support: Do I visit people at their work when the team is apart? Do I then represent to the individual the whole team in my manner and encouragement?

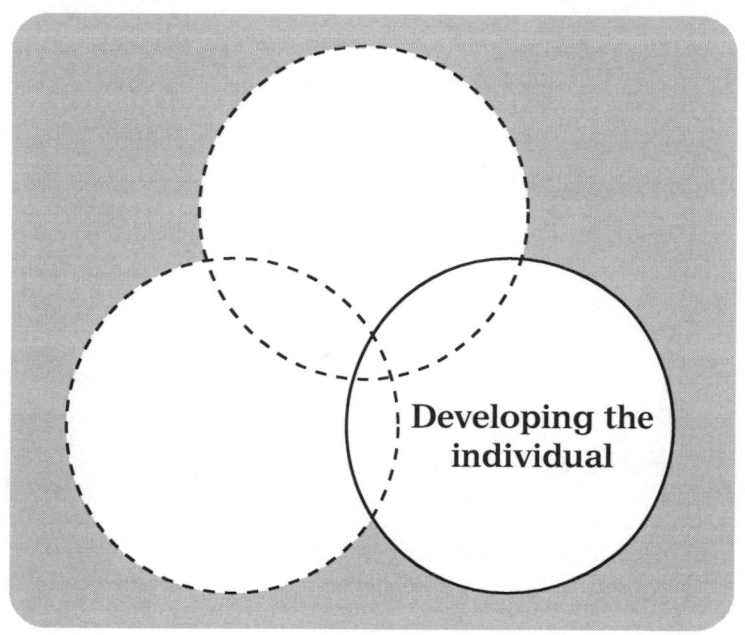

Developing the individual

Individual

Targets: Have they been agreed and quantified?

Induction: Does s/he really know the other team members and the organisation?

Achievement: Does s/he know how his/her work contributes to the overall result?

Responsibilities: Has s/he got a clear and accurate job description? Can I delegate more to him/her?

Authority: Does s/he have sufficient authority for his/her task?

Training: Has adequate provision been made for training or retraining both technical and as a team member?

Recognition: Do I emphasise people's successes? In failure is criticism constructive?

Growth: Does s/he see the chance of development? Does s/he see some pattern of career?

Performance: Is this regularly reviewed?

Reward: Are work, capacity and pay in balance?

The task: Is s/he in the right job? Has s/he the necessary resources?

The person: Do I know this person well? What makes him/her different from others?

Time/attention: Do I spend enough with individuals listening, developing and counselling?

Grievances: Are these dealt with promptly?

Security: Does s/he know about pensions, redundancy and so on?

Appraisal: Is the overall performance of each individual regularly reviewed in face-to-face discussion?

PART TWO

MOTIVATION

Motivation

Motivation is about something within you impelling you to move forwards, to achieve a goal, to make progress in a task. The 'something' which is the driving force may be a need, or a desire, or an emotion but it leads you to act in a certain way. Signs of motivation in a person are an energy and determination to achieve.

Typical qualities of a motivated person include:

- A willingness to work
- Dedication to the project or common cause
- Alignment of the person with the organisational goals
- Commitment
- An appetite to achieve
- An energy
- Drive and determination
- Tenacity
- Strength of purpose
- Orientation to work.

To be able to get the best from people, to achieve results through individuals and teams and to maintain consistent high performance, is all about inspiring oneself and others into action – this all depends on the skills of motivation and leadership.

Self-motivation can be as difficult as motivating others and you cannot have one without the other.

Understanding what moves an individual to action is crucial in a manager being able to engage the persons will to act. Motives (which operate the will which leads to action) are inner needs or desires and these can be conscious, semi-conscious or unconscious. We can be driven forwards by more than one motive at a time. In other words, motives can be mixed, with several clustered around a primary motive. We may not always know what out motives are, even though we are able to feel them, we cannot always label them. Sometimes we attribute our actions to credible motives (rationalisation) without realising what the true (usually unconscious) motives are. With this in mind it makes it quite difficult to think clearly about motivation as much of it can be unconscious.

To motivate others means to provide an incentive for them to do something, to initiate their behaviour and to stimulate them into activity. This can be done by infusing them with your own spirit, sense of achievement and motivational thoughts. You can improve your ability to inspire and motivate other people by:

- **Understanding what motivates you and others at work**: if you have a clear picture of what motivates you, you will be able to better understand what motivates others.

- **Being aware of different dimensions of motivation**: you can easily learn the generalisations about people and how to motivate them, but you need to remember that each individual person is unique and will therefore respond to different stimulants.

- **Developing your skills as a leader**: part of the role of being a manager is the ability to lead. This ability to lead means what you 'do' as a leader, and includes motivating and inspiring your team.

Adair's eight rules in motivating people

1 Be motivated yourself

2 Select people who are highly motivated

3 Treat each person as an individual

4 Set realistic and challenging targets

5 Remember that progress motivates

6 Create a motivating environment

7 Provide fair rewards

8 Give recognition

The 50:50 rule

Just as the Pareto principle (or 80:20 rule) is the ratio of 'the vital few and trivial many', the Adair 50:50 rule has it that:

50% of motivation comes from within a person; and

50% from his or her environment, especially from the leadership encountered therein.

Unfortunately, human behaviour and what decides/triggers it is more complicated than the carrot and stick 'theory' which deals only with external stimuli – providing rewards or punishments. The 'carrot' of reward/incentive and the 'stick' of fear of consequences reveal only two 'motives' which govern action. There are many more!

The expectancy theory – formulated by Edward C Tolman in the 1930s – (whereby behaviour rests on the instinctive tendency for individuals to balance the value of expected benefits against the expenditure of energy) falls into the same 'stimulus-response' approach to motivation. It demonstrates that an individual's strength of motivation can be affected by the expectations of outcomes from certain actions *and* further strengthened by the individuals preferred outcome, as demonstrated by Victor H. Vroom in the 1960s. Individuals are consciously self-interested in the outcomes of their actions. For example, a worker may put in extra time and effort to a project and expect to get paid more money. That is his desired reward and what he expects. If he doesn't receive what he expects his motivational level will fall dramatically.

Elton Mayo, in the Hawthorne experiments concluded that individuals adjusted their motivational levels to fit in with the group. The individual values the approval and acceptance of others and will conform to the groups motivational standards in order to 'fit in'.

One important point about expectancy theory is that individual perceptions can be very different, and the motivation and behaviour of individuals will vary considerably.

It pays, therefore, in external stimuli to bear in mind that:

1 **the routes to desired outcomes for individuals and teams are clear; and**

2 **individuals perceive the rewards or punishments in different ways according to their own values.**

There is a great need to treat people as individuals but as the 50:50 rule also indicates, other motivational factors should always be set in the context of the individual's managed environment. Leaders have a vital role to play in creating a motivational environment in which their team members can excel by in turn using the motivation within themselves. To be able to do this, we as leaders need to begin by looking at ourselves and getting our contribution right before we can criticise others.

The act of motivating someone means trying to change the direction of their motive energy. This can be consciously or unconsciously. As humans we are dependent on others for part of our motivation but we must be careful not to use this for our own benefit, this would be manipulation – a control over someone for unfair or insidious means. We should always act for the common purpose, rather than for our own purpose.

Motivation should not be confused with manipulation which can be about strong personalities dominating weaker ones. Good leaders respect the integrity of others and base their relationships on mutual trust, support, a sense of justice and a belief in the common cause.

Needs and motivation

Maslow's hierarchy of needs

Abraham Maslow suggests that a person is motivated by an inner programme of needs rather than by external motives such as rewards or punishments. When one of these sets of needs is met we move onto the next. Maslow thought that once a need is met it can no longer be a motivator. Human beings have a characteristic of always desiring something so once one need is fulfilled we automatically move onto the next, and so on.

A sketch map of individual needs – which is useful for managers when considering individuals – can be drawn from Maslow's hierarchy of needs (1954), but it must be borne in mind that his theory does not fully appreciate individual differences or that each person has a unique set of needs and values.

Maslow identified five motivating factors in his hierarchy of needs:

1 **Physiological needs (including hunger, thirst and sleep)**

2 **Safety needs (security and protection from danger)**

3 **Social needs (belonging, acceptance, social life, friendship and love)**

4 **Self-esteem (self-respect, achievement, status and recognition)**

5 **Self-actualisation (growth, accomplishment and personal development).**

However, points to bear in mind:

- Individuals do not necessarily move up the hierarchy on the principle that a 'satisfied need ceases to motivate' although that can be the case. Just because the social needs have been met doesn't automatically mean that you move on to the esteem needs.

- Different levels of needs can kick in at random points on the scale toward the full satisfaction of all the needs. For example, our physiological and security needs are more basic and if we are threatened we would move down the ladder to defend ourselves.

- Culture, age and other factors can affect the importance of the different needs to different people, and at different stages in their lives.

- The satisfying of some needs can be sacrificed in order to try and satisfy higher level needs. For example, some people would be willing to go without the more basic needs in order to fulfil their needs for achievement and recognition.

- Each person will have individual differences and unique sets of needs which will change at different stages of their lives.

Despite these points the hierarchy can still be useful to the leader in considering each of the team members and their motivational priorities.

McGregor's Theory X and Theory Y

In 1960 in his book, 'The Human Side of Enterprise', McGregor demonstrated that the way in which managers manage depends on the assumptions made about human behaviour. He grouped these assumptions into Theory X and Theory Y.

THEORY X – THE TRADITIONAL VIEW OF DIRECTION AND CONTROL

i) The average human being has an inherent dislike of work and will avoid it if possible.

ii) Because of this dislike of work, most people must be coerced, controlled, directed or threatened with punishment to get them to give adequate effort toward the achievement of organisational objectives; and

iii) The average human being prefers to be directed, wishes to avoid responsibility, has relatively little ambition and wants security above all.

THEORY Y – THE INTEGRATION OF INDIVIDUAL AND ORGANISATIONAL GOALS

i) The expenditure of physical and mental effort in work is as natural as play or rest.

ii) External control and the threat of punishment are not the only means for bringing about effort toward organisational objectives. People will exercise self-direction and self-control in the service of objectives to which they are committed.

iii) Commitment to objectives is a function of the rewards associated with their achievement.

iv) The average human being learns, under proper conditions, not only to accept but to seek responsibility.

v) The capacity to exercise a relatively high degree of imagination, ingenuity and creativity in the solution of organisational problems is widely, not narrowly, distributed in the population.

vi) Under the conditions of modern industrial life, the intellectual potentialities of the average human being are only partially utilised.

McGregor drew on Maslow for much of Theory Y and put forward the cluster of features as an unproven hypothesis and further research was needed (Herzberg) to seek to prove it correct.

In terms of management in practice, Theory Y does reveal that in any individual within an organisation there are untapped resources of goodwill, energy, creativity and intelligence. Everyone is a potential success at something – it just depends on their motivation and the motivation of others around them, to fulfil that potential.

Herzberg's Motivation – hygiene theory

Herzberg made the claim that people who are satisfied with their jobs were motivated by the need for achievement, recognition, self-actualisation and the like. By strengthening these motivators managers would allow their teams to have more job enrichment. He also noted that there are some factors which are 'satisfiers' and some factors which are 'dissatisfiers'.

In his research (published in his 1959 book 'The Motivation to Work'), fourteen factors were identified to be the sources of good or bad feelings (satisfiers or dissatisfiers):

1   Recognition

2   Achievement

3   Possibility of growth

4   Advancement

5   Salary

6   Interpersonal relations

7   Supervision – technical

8   Responsibility

9   Company policy and administration

10 Working conditions

11 Work itself

12 Factors in personal life

13 Status

14 Job security

The eight **'hygiene'** factors, according to Herzberg, which can create job dissatisfaction are:

1   **COMPANY POLICY AND ADMINISTRATION**
- Availability of clearly defined policies, especially those relating to people
- Adequacy of organisation and management

2   **SUPERVISION – TECHNICAL**
- Accessibility, competence and fairness of your superior

3 INTERPERSONAL RELATIONS

- Relations with supervisors, subordinates and colleagues
- Quality of the social life at work

4 SALARY

- The total compensation package, such as wages, salary, pension, company car and other financially related benefits

5 STATUS

- A person's position or rank in relation to others, symbolised by title, size of office or other tangible elements

6 JOB SECURITY

- Freedom from insecurity, such as loss of position or loss of employment altogether

7 PERSONAL LIFE

- The effect of a person's work on their family life, e.g. stress, unsocial hours or moving house

8 WORKING CONDITIONS

- The physical conditions in which you work
- The amount of work
- Facilities available
- Environmental aspects, e.g. ventilation, light, space, tools, noise

The six **motivating** factors that lead to job satisfaction were identified by Herzberg as being:

1   ACHIEVEMENT
- Specific successes, such as the successful completion of a job, solutions to problems, vindication and seeing the results of your work

2   RECOGNITION
- any act of recognition, whether notice or praise (separating recognition and reward from recognition with no reward)

3   POSSIBILITY OF GROWTH
- changes in job where professional growth potential is increased

4   ADVANCEMENT
- changes which enhance position or status at work

5   RESPONSIBILITY
- being given real responsibility, matched with necessary authority to discharge it

6   THE WORK ITSELF
- the actual doing of the job or phases of it.

Herzberg found that the satisfiers relate to the actual job in hand, whereas the dissatifiers are related to the job situation, the surrounds of the job, the working environment. If these factors which surround the job are not right they can course dissatisfaction which can lead to a low level of motivation, although not always so. However, even if they are right they are very weak motivators in their own right. It is the responsibility of a manager to make sure these hygiene factors are met, as a neglect of them may lead to a lack of success.

Satisfaction of the Herzberg motivators and avoidance of problems with the hygiene factors can help you as a manager to assess roles and jobs within your organisation, and to check what job-enrichment or empowerment you ought to contemplate to improve performance and give individuals greater job satisfaction.

Checklist: Hygiene factors

- Is your working environment clean and pleasant?

  _____

  _____

- Are the noise levels acceptable?

  _____

  _____

- Is there a good record of health and safety?

  _____

  _____

- Is there a place away from the main working environment dedicated to smoking?

  _____

  _____

- Do the workforce have all the tools and equipment to be able to carry out their jobs effectively?

  _____

  _____

- Are social activities encouraged amongst staff?

  _____

  _____

- Are changes within the workplace and changes to working practice handled in a sensitive way?

  _____

  _____

- Do the staff have a sense of security within their jobs?

  _____

  _____

- Are their training programmes available to help people to advance their learning?

  _____

  _____

- Are salaries and rewards perceived as fair?

  _____

  _____

- Is there a feeling of working in a team as opposed to a 'them and us' structure?

  _____

  _____

- Has anyone in the organisation been demoted without good reason?

  _____

  _____

The three circles model

There are three areas within a working organisation: the need to accomplish the common task, the needs of the team for unity and the needs of the individual, both human and personal. These three areas overlap and because they each have their own motivational forces they can interact both positively and negatively.

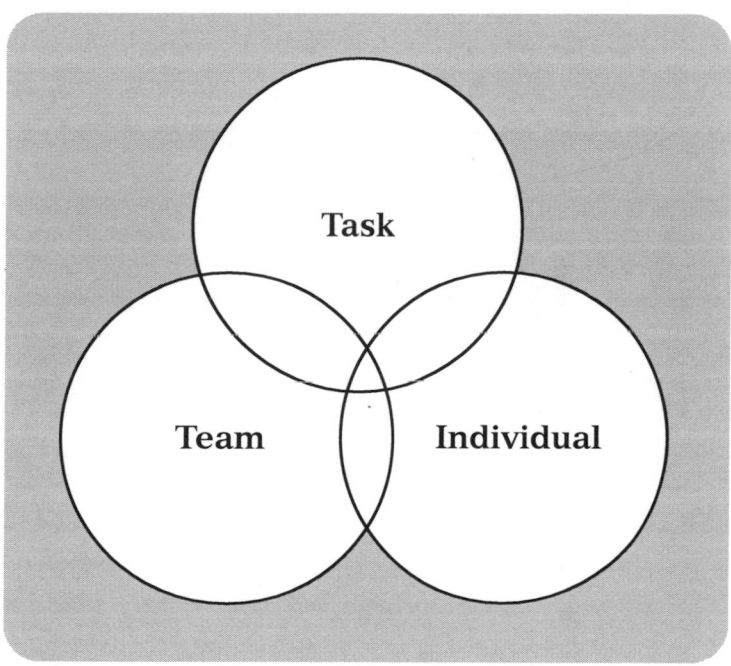

Examples of positive interaction:

- Achievement of a common task builds a sense of team unity and boosts morale.

- Good internal communications and a vibrant team spirit developed from previous successes make a group more likely to achieve common tasks more effectively. This in turn gives the individual a morale boost.

- If an individual is recognised for their input and contribution to both the task and the team, they are more likely to be motivated in both these areas to succeed again.

Examples of negative interaction:

- If a team fails in its task this will lead to negative feelings both within the group and within each individual.

- If there is a lack of team spirit and relationships aren't good between team members this will affect job performance and also individual needs.

- If individuals aren't happy in their environment and in their work they will not be motivated to make their best contributions to achieving the common task or to the spirit of the group.

The meeting of individual needs is dependant on the two other areas:

- Physiological needs such as food and water are met by earning money through doing the task, which allows us to buy the necessary supplies for ourselves and our families.

- Safety/security needs can be met through having a permanent job which allows you to earn money, which can be used for insurance and pensions – financial security. There is also a certain amount of security felt by working in a team which you trust.

- Social needs can be met by the camaraderie found in the workplace and the team spirit generated in achieving the common task. Relationships with long-term suppliers also contribute to the social needs.

- Esteem needs are also met when the common task is achieved as this gives the individual a sense of self-confidence, self-respect and recognition from others.

- Self-actualisation is a by-product of commitment to an important task which pushes your abilities to the limit.

Managers/leaders and motivation

Managers and leaders should take a realistic and visionary view of people who work for them and with them. Individuals can be managed better if it is recognised that they are:

1   individuals, but become fully developed and truly themselves in relation to other people and meaningful work;

2   creative and imaginative, but only in concert with others through working on their own or in teams;

3   driven by achievement (as individuals) but know that they achieve more as part of a team;

4   self-motivated and self-directed but need management/ leadership (if only to co-ordinate activities);

5   intelligent enough to know the difference between rewards such as money and those less tangible rewards that meet value needs; and

6   interested in leaving work/the world a better place than they found it and know that that yields an inestimable bonus.

As a manager and leader it is your responsibility to meet the three areas of need:

- Achieving the task
- Building and maintaining the team
- Motivating and developing the individual.

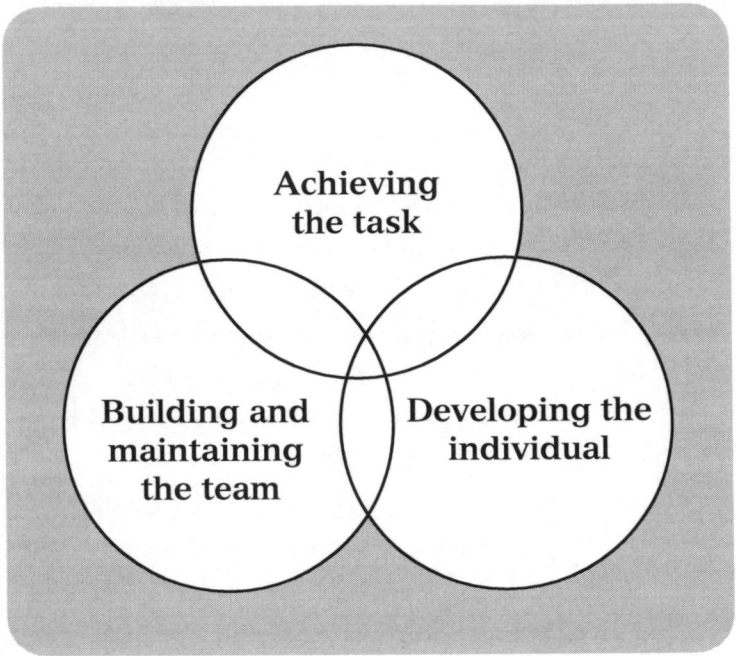

The achievement of the task, the building and maintaining of the team and the development of the individual can only result from motivating people by providing the leadership functions of:

- Planning
- Initiating
- Controlling

- Supporting

- Informing

- Evaluating

and by being able to inspire others.

Motivation is the result of performing all these functions well.

Managers should check that individuals have:

1   a sense of achievement in their job and feel that they are making a worthwhile contribution to the objective of the team

2   jobs which are challenging and demanding with responsibilities to match their capabilities

3   adequate recognition for their achievements

4   control over their delegated duties

5   a feeling that they are developing along with their growing experience and ability.

Motivation and decision-making

The more that people are involved in making the decisions that affect them, the more they are likely to be motivated to carry them out. However, there are always situational factors that can limit the amount of involvement possible:

- The nature of the task

- The time available

- The attitudes, knowledge and experience of the individuals

- The personality of the leader

- The philosophy of the organisation.

Even if it is not possible to involve the team in making a decision, for example in a crisis situation, it is usually possible to involve them to some degree in the means of carrying out the decision – i.e. methods, techniques, conditions and plans.

Manager's motivating checklist
DO YOU

- Agree with subordinates their main targets and responsibilities together with standards of performance, so that you can both recognise achievement?

  _____

  _____

- Recognise the contribution of each member of the team and encourage team members to do the same?

  _____

  _____

- Acknowledge success and build on it?

  _____

  _____

- Analyse set-backs; identifying what went well and giving constructive guidance to improve future performance?

  _____

  _____

- Delegate as much as possible giving more discretion over decisions and accountability to a sub-group or individual?

  _____

  _____

- Show those that work with you that you trust them, or do you surround them with unnecessary controls?

  _____

  _____

- Provide adequate opportunities for training and re-training if necessary?

  _____

  _____

- Encourage each individual to develop his/her capacities to the full?

  _____

  _____

- Review the overall performance of each individual regularly face-to-face?

  _____

  _____

- Match financial reward to contribution?

  _____

  _____

- Make time to talk and listen so that you understand the unique and changing profile of needs and wants in each person, and work with what you find?

  _____

  _____

- Encourage able people with the prospect of promotion within the organisation?

  _____

  _____

Getting the best from people

There are seven important strategies you should consider and put into practice if you want to get the best out of the people who work for and with you:

- Be motivated yourself
- Select people who are or who have the potential to be highly motivated
- Treat each person as an individual with individual needs
- Set challenging but realistic targets and tasks
- Remember that progress and achievement motivates
- Provide fair rewards linked to progress and achievement
- Give recognition publicly when it is due.

By using these seven strategies you will have a clear sense of direction towards creating a high-performance team. You will also be better equipped to help your organisation transform itself into a stimulating and motivating place to work.

Let's look at each of the seven strategies in turn.

Be motivated yourself

You will never be able to inspire others if you do not feel inspired yourself. Enthusiasm is infectious, and when it's combined with commitment and trust it's a great example as a motivator to others.

To be able to be a good example to others you should be:

- **Public:** make sure you act in the open so those around you can see where you are coming from and where you are going

- **Spontaneous:** do not appear calculated, act naturally, show people your genuine character

- **Expressive:** do things because they are natural to you, not for effect as this can be counter-effective

- **Self-effacing:** setting a good example is not glory-seeking, you shouldn't expect attention from it.

In terms of motivating others your own commitment is paramount. Showing and practising commitment to the task, the team and each individual will get you results. As Ghandi once said, "We must be the change we wish to see in the world".

Motivation is contagious so you should be infectious! If you are not motivated yourself, you cannot motivate others and you should examine the reasons why you lack motivation. Symptoms include:

- Having little or no interest in the job
- Having a sense of not fitting in and being out of place
- Avoiding talking about your job
- Wanting to arrive laté and leave early
- Wanting to leave the job and having an active dislike for it.

You should feel that you have found your vocation and the best way to put your talents to good use. You will have a sense of enjoyment and fun in doing your work, not of toil or drudgery. This doesn't mean that you won't encounter problems but you will have lots of motivation to overcome them.

Checklist: Are you doing the right job?

- Do you enjoy the majority of your work?

  _____

  _____

- Do you have one outstanding talent that you can name without thinking too hard?

  _____

  _____

- Has that talent been recognised by others around you, by reward or promotion?

  _____

  _____

- Did you discover it in your early years at work? (Specific talents usually become known quite early on.)

  _____

  _____

- Can you identify the key talents of those around you?

  _____

  _____

- Does you work continually stretch your abilities?

  _____

  _____

- Would you consider taking a cut in pay to do a job which used your specific talents?

  _____

  _____

- Would you pay for a training course to help develop your natural talents?

  _____

  _____

You can strengthen your motivation by reminding yourself:

1 to feel and act enthusiastically and in a committed way in your work

2 to take responsibility when things go wrong rather than blaming others

3   to identify ways you can lead by example

4   act on the 50:50 principle

5   to motivate by word and example rather than manipulation

6   to set an example naturally rather than in a calculated way
     and never ask someone to do something you would not
     do yourself

7   not to give up easily

8   to ensure you are in the right job for your own abilities,
     interests and temperament

9   to be able to cite experiences where what you have said
     or done has had an inspirational effect on individuals, the
     team or the organisation

10   that the three badges of leadership are enthusiasm, commit-
     ment and perseverance.

Select people who are highly motivated

Recruiting people who are already highly motivated is not that
simple. Remember the 50:50 rule – the extent to which you can
motivate someone is limited, for 50 per cent of their motivation has to come from within themselves and is therefore in
their hands. When you select someone for a job it is better to
choose someone who is highly motivated but has modest talent,
rather than the very talented with little or no motivation. If
the motivation is present they will leap to the challenge of developing their talents.

The seven key indicators of high motivation in an individual
are:

1   **Energy**: not necessarily shown in an extrovert way but with
     an alertness and quiet resolve

2   **Commitment**: consider if the person appears to be willing to commit to the common purpose

3   **Staying power**: consider if in the face of problems, difficulties or set-backs this person would stick with it or give up too easily

4   **Skill**: the possession of skills indicates aims and ambitions, possibly in a certain direction

5   **Single-mindedness**: a person who pushes their energy in a single direction is likely to be more motivated than a butterfly who flits from one job arena to another

6   **Enjoyment**: if a person does not enjoy their job and find some fun in it they will not be motivated. Enjoyment goes hand in hand with motivation

7   **Responsibility**: a willingness to seek and accept responsibility is a person who wants to advance themselves and has the motivation to do so.

Choosing people well (and if mistakes are made they should be confronted and remedied early) means looking at motivation, ability and personality and you should, when interviewing, look for real evidence behind the interviewee's facade. Every team member should be motivated, not just the managers or staff dealing directly with customers.

In the interview situation remember:

*   The interviewee is trying to get you to give them the job. Some people find it quite easy to appear very enthusiastic and highly motivated in the time of an interview. Others who are much more genuinely motivated may not be at their best in the interview situation and appear to be very laid back.

- Look for evidence of enthusiasm and motivation within their past experiences. Talk to the referees who know them well to find out more about them.

- In the interview ask the applicant how they would react in certain situations that would require high motivation and analyse their answers carefully.

Looking for the Michelangelo motive (where the quality of the work itself is a key motivator) can yield good results in selecting highly motivated individuals. You should make a point of looking for:

- A sense of pride in the individual's own work

- An attention to detail

- A willingness to 'walk the extra mile' to get things right

- A total lack of the 'its good enough, let it go' mentality

- An inner direction or responsibility for the work (without the need for supervision)

- An ability to assess and evaluate their own work, independently from the opinions of others.

It should be stressed that perfectionism is not what is called for – the best can be the enemy of the good.

Managers should check whether individuals are in the right job with the right skills and abilities, otherwise motivation techniques will fail. The aim is to select people who are motivated for the most appropriate job.

Checklist: Selecting people who are motivated

- Do you have team members who are under-motivated and therefore not performing at their best?

  _____

  _____

- Do you review your selection procedures on a regular basis?

  _____

  _____

- Do you have accurate ways of assessing potential employees for motivation, ability and personality within the interview time?

  _____

  _____

- How do you assess if candidates have the Michelangelo motive?

  _____

  _____

- Do outside clients and suppliers talk about the high level of motivation within your organisation?

  _____

  _____

- Does your organisation have a high level of staff turnover? If so, can you identify why?

  _____

  _____

Treat each person as an individual

Find out what motivates an individual, do not rely on generalised theories or assumptions. Each individual is just that, individual. Not all individuals will be clear about what motivates them. It is part of your responsibility as a leader to find out what 'makes them tick'. By entering into a dialogue with each team member you can help them to clarify what it is that motivates them – and use what you find to your mutual benefit.

Also, remember to treat each individual as a person, not just a manager, worker, customer etc.

In each person you should engender a sense of:

- **Trust**: productive communication does not happen until some form of trust is present.
- **Autonomy**: every individual needs a sense of belonging but also a sense of self-sufficiency, of being in control.
- **Initiative**: initiative can be developed. It is the power that moves people to start something.
- **Industry**: work which has a feeling of purpose about it develops this sense of industry which is vital both in and out of the workplace.
- **Integrity**: this is about conforming to standards and values outside of oneself. It helps us create a sense of wholeness about our being.
- **Security**: not just job security but also a feeling of security within the team and from other significant people.

It is important for a leader to spend time with individuals, not just with the team as a whole. There are few things as motivating as personal attention. It gives the individual a sense of importance within their own right as well as within the team. Also one-to-one sessions give the leader a chance to coach or counsel their staff which allows them to develop as team members, as well as individuals. By spending more time with individuals you will be much more aware of when their motivation or morale is flagging, and be able to help them get back on track before the feelings get out of hand. You will also be more aware of when they are due some praise or constructive criticism and be able to administer it at the appropriate time.

Individuals can often be vulnerable if they, or the team as a whole, don't succeed at a task. People suffer when they are subjected to repeated failures, criticisms, frustrations or defeats. By being more in touch with them you will be able to reassure, inspire and make them believe in themselves again. These are the skills of a good team leader.

Take time with each individual to:

Encourage:

- Give hope, courage and confidence, accompanied by help if necessary
- Inspire and urge along
- Stimulate an individual with the promise of a reward, and make sure they receive if they achieve the goal

Hearten:

- Give fresh courage if someone is flagging
- Renew their spirit

Inspire:

- Infuse them with confidence and enthusiasm
- Guide them
- Animate them with good feelings of being able to achieve

Support:

- Give them help if they are in need to get them back on track
- Guide them until they can stand alone again

Embolden:

- Give them the confidence for them to believe in their ability
- Impart courage on them

Stimulate:

- Prod or goad them into the right form of action
- Incite them into doing a task

Remember, each individual matters and is important, both in their own right and as members of the team, to be able to achieve the common task.

Checklist: Do you treat each person as an individual?

- Do you know the names of the people on your team and their teams if they are leaders?

  _____

  _____

- Can you identify ways in which those who report to you differ from each other?

  _____

  _____

- Do you accept that what motivates an individual can and will change, depending on the influences in their lives at the time?

  _____

  _____

- Do you spend individual time with people to get to know them, work with them, coach and support them when necessary?

  _____

  _____

- Does the organisation respond flexibly to changes in circumstances outside of the workplace which may affect the individual during working hours?

  _____

  _____

- Does your organisation see you as an individual, not just a leader?

  _____

  _____

Set realistic and challenging targets

One of your main aims as a leader is to understand the organisation's aims and purposes. By understanding the common task you will be able to break it down into areas of purpose, and then targets and objectives can be identified. These are the attainable steps which a team can focus on to achieve the desired result without becoming overwhelmed by the enormity of the whole task.

The PURPOSE is the common task at hand. AIMS are about the direction of the effort in one or more areas of the common task. The OBJECTIVES are tangible, specific, attainable and towards which the effort is directed.

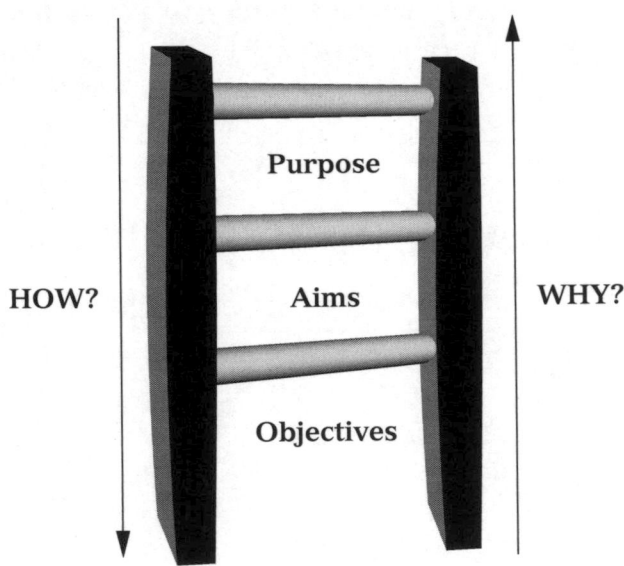

Jacobs ladder

Jacob's ladder model

Moving **down** the ladder, ask 'How are we going to achieve the task?'

The answer is by breaking down the purpose into the main aims, and the main aims into short and long-term objectives or goals.

Moving **up** the ladder, ask 'Why are we doing this?' The answer is to achieve this objective in order to achieve this aim and to satisfy this purpose or achieve the common task.

Targets set, for both short and longer-term objectives, should be:

- specific;
- clear; and
- time-bounded.

An objective or target must be realistic (feasible) and challenging. If you aim for the best you can often get it. A challenging task should test your abilities, powers and resources to the full. It should not be threatening but stimulating, provocative, inspiring and, above all, motivating. But, remember that everybody is an individual and what challenges one person may be far too daunting for another. There is no benefit in setting unrealistic targets as they will not inspire or motivate people. If they cannot be met, why bother trying in the first place? On the other hand, if they are too easy to attain they will not be inspirational or motivational. It is up to the leader and their management skills to be able to get the balance just right.

If possible, targets should be agreed with those who will be trying to achieve them. If a person accepts the target and the required objective as being realistic, even if it is challenging, they are more likely to want to succeed at achieving it and will be committed to doing so. They will draw upon the 50 per cent of their motivation which comes from within.

However, it is not always possible to involve the team in making decisions. As a leader you need to consider the ability, maturity and experience of the team when deciding whether or not to ask for their participation. Also, sometimes there may not be enough time for others to be consulted. It may be a crisis situation where every minute counts. If you, as a leader, involve your team as often and as much as possible, subject to the limits of the task, time and circumstances imposed on you, you will gain the respect of those you need the commitment and motivation from. This will stand you in good stead in the times when you are unable to involve them in the decision-making process.

Checklist: Do you set realistic and challenging targets?

- Are you clear about your team's objectives for them to be able to achieve the common task or target?

  _____

  _____

- Have you agreed the targets with them and gained their commitment to the task in hand?

  _____

  _____

- Can you clearly see how these targets relate to the purpose of the organisation as a whole?

  _____

  _____

- Are the targets realistic and feasible in the time limits set?

  _____

  _____

- Are the targets challenging but not too daunting?

  _____

  _____

- Are the targets challenging but not too simple?

  _____

  _____

- Are the targets related to both short and long-term goals?

  _____

  _____

- Do you encourage your team to set their own targets and goals?

  _____

  _____

Remember that progress motivates

There is a 'lust to finish' (John Wesley) and the key principle is that progress motivates. We are motivated, not just our own progress in meeting our individual needs, but also in meeting the needs of the group emanating from the commitment of achieving the common task. If people know and feel that they are moving forwards they tend to put in more effort. Human beings like to succeed.

Feedback on the progress made is crucial. Without feedback people don't know if they are making progress or not. Progress (or even the relative lack of progress) helps motivation – either to spur people on or to concentrate the mind on what yet needs to be done to achieve the desired outcome.

Sometimes feedback is given in a negative, criticising way as a means of expressing annoyance or anger. This does nothing positive for the feeling of motivation within a team or an individual.

Feedback is sometimes inaccurate, not given at all or not often enough, usually for these reasons:

- 'People don't need to be told how they are doing, they already know'

- 'People take it easy and become complacent if you say things are going well'

- 'They are unhappy and cause trouble if you say things are not going well'

- 'We lack the skills or the time to do it effectively'

- 'It's not one of our priorities so we don't spend time doing it'

- 'It's not seen as relevant to the job in hand'.

Giving feedback and information on progress has the effect of 'topping up' motivational levels. By giving praise for a job well done or a task successfully completed, you are helping individuals and teams to build on their strengths and take steps towards further progress. Praise is a great morale and motivation booster. Improvement suggestions or constructive criticism, handled in the correct way and given at the appropriate time, helps to maintain performance levels. It allows people and teams to continue to move in the right direction with confidence despite difficulties or set backs. It is easy to criticise and sometimes we spend too much time doing that rather than praising the achievements, however small. Remember though, don't praise without reason otherwise it becomes meaningless, empty and insincere and will not achieve the results you were hoping for.

Feedback which is affirmative (praise) must be:

- Accurate
- Sincere
- Generous
- Spontaneous
- Fair.

It must not be:

- Patronising
- Superior/condescending
- Grudging
- Calculated for effect.

Briefing the team about the tasks that lie ahead is an effective way of communicating your own enthusiasm and inspiration for the plan of action about to be embarked upon. This is a good time to energise and motivate the team, and lift their spirits.

Maintaining motivation depends on informing and inspiring, and the rule is always to give information first before you attempt to encourage. Remember, truth is the basis of inspiration. The reality of the situation is what motivates people, not you the leader. You are just the conveyor of that truth and reality.

Maintaining high morale is key to high motivation and covers the individuals and the team.

Morale is the mental and emotional attitude of an individual or a team, to the task or targets in hand. It is also about the sense of a common purpose and a respect within a team.

If you sense there is a drop in levels of morale you will need to identify if it is an individual who has problems or if it is coming from the team in general. How people relate to each other and talk amongst themselves creates a type of atmosphere which you will be able to pick up on.

Signs of low morale can be identified by listening out for remarks such as:

- 'We are on a losing streak'
- 'What good is all this extra effort doing?'
- 'Does anyone know where we're heading? We seem to be going round in circles'
- 'This industry has no future'
- 'The targets are unrealistic, we are beaten before we even start'
- 'We need better leader to direct us through this'
- 'The strategic plan is just something to keep head office busy'
- 'We are a second class organisation, we don't have a hope of competing against the others in our market'

These types of remarks are usually heard in informal settings, so that is where you should be looking out for them.

Where an individual has low morale, the issues have to be addressed on an individual basis, but where group or team morale is low, the answer lies in deciding whether there is a lack of confidence:

- of ultimate success
- in the present plan(s)
- in the leadership/management
- in the minds of team members.

It can be necessary to re-motivate the team by rebuilding self-confidence and by re-addressing:

- aims – and clarifying objectives
- plans, resources needed
- leadership
- overlooked factors

Also, think about the following areas of the task which may make a difference to morale:

- What is the value of the task(s) to those trying to achieve it?
- Are the objectives and purposes of the task clear to all those involved?
- Does everyone in the team understand why they have been asked to help achieve this task?
- Has the task been clearly broken down into aims and objectives?
- Are all the necessary tools and resources available for the achievement of the task to be possible?

- Is there good team leadership in place?

- Did the team and the individuals have an involvement in the key decision-making and planning stages?

- Should the present plan be changed or modified in light of new findings?

- Have any factors been overlooked that could make a difference to the structure of the plan?

Be certain to communicate any changes of direction or changes to the plan carefully and clearly to all those involved. If possible, allow the team to have an input into the decision-making process. This will boost their sense of belonging and value, and therefore heighten levels of morale. Let the team know that you believe in them, that you have confidence in them and that you know you can work together to get the project back on track. Do not give them false promises or hopes but do give them the truth – they will respect you for it and be motivated by it.

To create a motivating environment, remember the following points:

1. Beware of creating a restrictive organisation with an overemphasis on controls

2. Never criticise individuals publicly, do it in private and in a constructive manner

3. Ensure Herzberg's hygiene factors are catered for – the physical and psychological well-being of people should have high priority

4. Control systems should only be introduced where necessary

5. Give people an opportunity to input into the decisions which affect their working lives (especially in respect of substantial change)

6   Keep units and sub-units as small as possible (for large units tend to be bureaucratic and de-motivational if they lack inspired leaders)

7   Pay attention to job design – avoid repetitive work, introduce variety and avoid boredom and monotony

8   Give people autonomy and a job with a 'product' that an individual can recognise as his/her own

9   Ensure an individual understands the significance of their job in relation to the whole, which will also encourage new ideas and innovation.

Checklist: Do you use progress as a tool for motivation?

- Do you actively encourage people while they are involved in a task?

  _____

  _____

- Do you give regular feedback about progress to individuals?

  _____

  _____

- Do you give regular feedback about progress to the team?

  _____

  _____

- Do you take an overall view of the team and task in hand, and evaluate levels of morale throughout?

  _____

  _____

- Is morale an important attribute to you and your team?

  _____

  _____

- Do you and your team see the organisation as an inspirational one?

  _____

  _____

- Are you able to identify when morale is falling and act effectively to get it back on track?

  _____

  _____

- If things become difficult are you still able to provide enough encouragement to your team to keep them motivated?

  _____

  _____

Provide fair rewards

Money is a key incentive for the majority of people. Although it is difficult to ensure that the financial reward an individual receives is fair (commensurate with contribution), effort must be applied in trying to get it right. If there is a lack of fairness this will lead very quickly to a lack of motivation and low morale. Also, if monetary rewards are too low they will be seen by workers as insulting and will lead to less effort being put into the job.

There are other motivating 'returns' that individuals look for from jobs (as in Maslow's hierarchy of needs), such as professional development and personal growth opportunities. Also of tactical importance are incentives to improve performance in key areas, e.g. sales, customer service and credit control.

Remember the value of money as a motivator will depend on an individual's circumstances and expectations. These will vary from individual to individual. However, money and its various functions is important to everyone to some degree:

- **Means of exchange:** it is the means by which we get food, shelter and other things needed for our survival.

- **Store of wealth:** we save money, not just to stock pile wealth, but to secure our futures when we are no longer able to earn a salary.

- **Basis for comparison:** we see money as a basis for comparing ourselves to others, our level of career success is often shown by the amount of money we earn.

- **Means of recognition:** a reward or prize is perceived as a means of recognition for a job well done.

- **All-embracing:** not only does money provide us with the basic needs of food and shelter it also provides us with a means of educating ourselves and our children, by schooling, travel, socialising etc.

Salaries should be in-line with performance and responsibilities. A good salary will motivate people but an above average salary for the job will not necessarily give you an above average performance in return. However, a poor salary will cause dissatisfaction and de-motivation. A good motivator for most individuals is the combination of a fixed salary with a variable element related to performance or profits. The fixed salary allows people to 'know' they can pay the mortgage and food bills etc., whereas the variable part gives the individual a sense of motivation and achievement, if they manage to earn it.

A drawback of performance related pay is the problem of allocating it. Should the whole organisation be rewarded? If so, should different amounts go to different ranks? Would it be more appropriate to reward a particular team? Or should it be allocated to one particular individual? Be aware that if you get it wrong you could divide a team and create a lot of bad feeling. A key is to keep performance related pay structures as simple as possible and as fair as possible.

Profit sharing is a strategic way of relating performance to pay. It is also a great way to get commitment from workers as they feel they are really part of the organisation. From the employers point of view there are no payouts if there are no profits.

Motivating by incentives is more tactical. It can be a good way of:

- Increasing productivity from a sales team
- Improving after sales customer service
- Increasing product knowledge amongst employees.

The incentives can be in the form of:

- **Cash:** this method is cost-effective and flexible, but:
  - it may make staff think managers are only concerned with money
  - staff may feel manipulated
  - it can look like an easy way out for staff to be rewarded
  - unless the amounts are substantial the cash will be frittered away and staff have nothing to show for it
  - many employees see money as their rightful reward, they shouldn't have to prove themselves to receive what they are worth, it should automatically be part of their salary
- **Vouchers:** this is easy for the employer to organise, but:
  - it can be seen as a less glamorous version of cash, depending on where the vouchers are from or what they are for
- **Merchandise:** this suggests real effort on the part of the employer, but:
  - employees may expect to be given a choice
  - this involves greater organisation, co-ordination and administration costs
- **Travel:** this is a great motivator in terms of perceived value and appeals to most people, but:
  - it is the most expensive option
  - it incurs high administrative costs and lots of organisation.

Care must be taken to administer any incentive schemes fairly with everyone having an equal opportunity to compete. Also, because there is the element of competition there will be winners and losers, great care must be taken not to de-motivate any 'losers'. Keep an incentive scheme as much fun as possible without losing the motivational effects of it.

Checklist: Does your organisation provide fair rewards?

- Do we have a scheme whereby financial reward is made up of a fixed and variable element?

  _____

  _____

- Do we link performance and pay?

  _____

  _____

- Do employees perceive the system of allocating rewards as fair and just?

  _____

  _____

- Have we addressed the problems of whether to pay performance-related elements to the organisation, team or the individual?

  _____

  _____

- Do we actively consider changing our information systems to improve methods of calculating and rewarding performance?

  _____

  _____

- Do we have schemes other than for sales people?

  _____

  _____

- Does our organisation reward the behaviour/
  performance that it publicly values?

  _____

  _____

- Do senior managers have pay rises/bonuses when
  they expect others to do without them?

  _____

  _____

It is always worth remembering Herzberg's insight that salary has more power to make people dissatisfied or unhappy than it has the power to motivate them. The motivational effects of a pay rise wear off after a period of time.

Give recognition

Everybody is receptive to positive recognition. Financial reward is seen by the recipient as a tangible form of recognition. There are other ways whereby appreciation is expressed for what has been contributed.

If recognition is not given, an individual can feel unnoticed, unvalued and unrewarded. This leads to a drop in motivation and energy levels. The power of recognition as a motivator should not be underestimated. Herzberg rated it highly as a factor in job satisfaction.

Recognition should be formal or informal, for the individual and/or the team, as appropriate.

In giving recognition, you should try to ensure that you:

1 Treat everyone in a fair and equal way

2 Reward real achievements or contributions

3 Reflect the core values of the organisation

4 Use it to guide and encourage all concerned

5 Give it in public if possible

6 Give it formally and informally

7 Give it genuinely and sincerely.

Being sincere is key when giving recognition. Remember also to give the recognition when it is due. When you see a reason for it say something there and then, don't wait until later as the impact of the moment may be lost. You may have to look for opportunities to give recognition as some people work very diligently and are high achievers but don't put themselves in the limelight to attract attention. They are likely to accept the compliment in an understated, quiet way but it would still be very much appreciated and highly motivating.

Make sure you recognise the people that carry out routine tasks consistently well. This is an achievement on their part and if it's not recognised they may begin to feel they are being taken for granted. Don't forget the receptionists, the security guard or the typist as they are the people that keep the organisation running smoothly. Everyone wants to feel they have a worth and they are appreciated for it.

Other than financial payments, any words of recognition could be reinforced by giving:

- Time off (with pay)
- Tickets for an event or dinner out
- Small gift
- Special project of importance
- A change in job title or a promotion.

It is a good idea to back-up words of praise or recognition with some tangible gift. If the team is to be recognised for an achievement, give them a budget and ask them for suggestions about what they would like to do to celebrate.

Find out what is going on, share praise received with subordinates and say thank you more often, because people really value positive recognition and are motivated by it.

Know people's names – that is the basic form of recognition!

Checklist: Do you give enough recognition?

- Do you know what is going on in your team to be able to give recognition to those who deserve it?

  _____

  _____

- If you are praised by your superiors do you pass that recognition on to your team members?

  _____

  _____

- Do you have the necessary skills to be able to praise effectively without being insincere?

  _____

  _____

- Do you know the names of everyone in your team?

  _____

  _____

- Does your organisation reinforce recognition with tangible gifts?

  _____

  _____

Summary

Teambuilding

Leaders should consider all the following issues if they are to build and maintain high-performance teams:

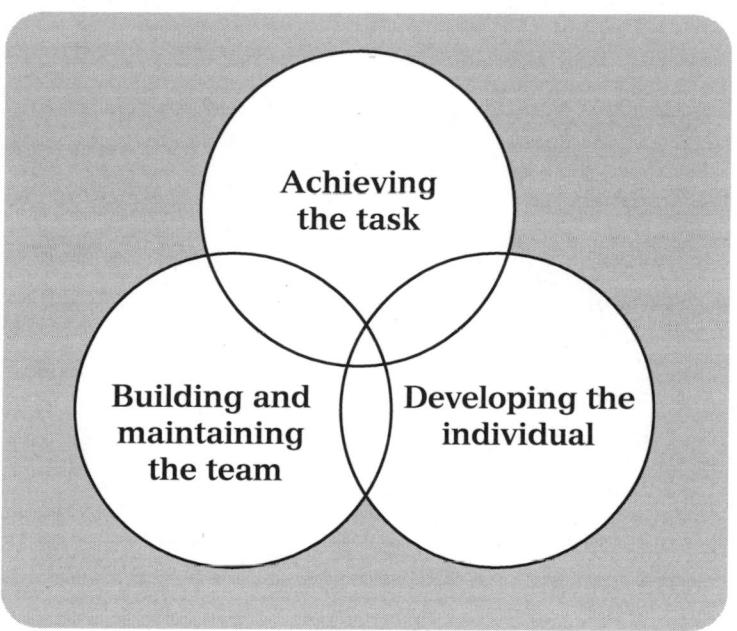

Achieving the task:

- Purpose
- Responsibilities
- Objectives
- Programme
- Working conditions
- Resources
- Targets
- Authority
- Training
- Priorities
- Progress
- Supervision
- Setting an example.

Building and maintaining the team:

- Objectives
- Standards
- Safety standards
- Size of team
- Team members
- Team spirit
- Discipline
- Grievances
- Consultation
- Briefing
- Representing
- Supporting.

Developing the individual:

- Targets
- Induction
- Achievement
- Responsibilities
- Authority
- Training
- Recognition
- Growth
- Performance
- Reward
- The task
- The person
- Time/attention
- Grievances
- Security
- Appraisal.

Motivation

To achieve a highly motivated team the leader should consider the following issues:

- Be motivated yourself
- Select people who are already motivated
- Set challenging but realistic targets
- Remember that progress motivates
- Treat each person as an individual
- Provide fair rewards
- Give recognition

Quotes about Teambuilding and Motivation

'You do not know me, I do not know you, but we have got to work together. Therefore, we must understand each other, we must have confidence in each other. I have only been here a few hours, but from what I have seen and heard since I arrived, I am prepared to say here and now that I have confidence in you. We will work together as a team. I believe that one of the first duties is to create what I call atmosphere. I do not like the general atmosphere I find here — it is an atmosphere of doubt, of looking back. All that must cease. I want to impress upon everyone that the bad times are over and it will be done. If anybody here thinks it cannot be done, let him go at once. I do not want any doubters. It can be done and it will be done beyond any possibility of doubt.'

FIELD MARSHAL VISCOUNT MONTGOMERY

Extract from speech to staff in taking over the Eighth Army before the Battle of El Alamein

MORALE

Morale
>Shows itself
>As a state of mind
>Radiating confidence
>In people

Where each member
>Feels sure of his own niche,
>Stands on his own abilities
>And works out his own solutions
>– Knowing he is
>Part of a team

Where no person
>Feels anxiety or fear
>Or pressure to be better
>Than someone else

Where there exists
>A sharing of ideas
>A freedom to plan
>A sureness of worth,
>And a knowledge
>That help is available
>For the asking

To the end that
>People grow and mature
>Warmed by a friendly climate

ANON

'Light is the task, when many share the toil.'

HOMER

'The two great movers of the human mind are the desire of good and the fear of evil.'

SAMUEL JOHNSON

'I am persuaded that every being
has a part to play on earth:
to be exact, his or her own part
which resembles no other.'

ANDRÉ GIDE

'Such is the state of life that none are happy but by
the anticipation of change.'

SAMUEL JOHNSON

'A man has one eye on what he gives, but seven eyes
on what he receives.'

OLD GERMAN PROVERB

'A man's reach should exceed his grasp.'

ROBERT BROWNING

'If you treat people as they are, they will stay as they are. But if you treat them as they ought to be, they will become bigger and better persons.'

GOETHE

'Give me a fire and I will give you light'

OLD ARAB PROVERB

'Nothing great was ever achieved without enthusiasm.'

EMERSON

'No man will find the best way to do a thing
unless he loves to do that thing.'   OLD JAPANESE PROVERB

'It is not enough to do our best. Sometimes we have to do what is required.'

CHURCHILL

'Management, above everything else, is about people.

It is about the accomplishment of ends and aims by

the efforts of groups of people working together.

The people and their individual hopes and skills are the

greatest variable and the most important one.'

SIR JOHN HARVEY-JONES

'You get more of the behaviour you reward.

You don't get what you hope for, ask for, wish for, or beg for.

You get what you reward.'   MICHEL LE BOEUF

'Fame is the spur that the clear spirit doth raise...

To scorn delights and live laborious days.'   MILTON

'Any of us will put out more and better ideas

if our efforts are fully appreciated.'   ALEXANDER F OSBORN

'No man does anything from a single motive.'

SAMUEL TAYLOR COLERIDGE

'BY ASKING THE
IMPOSSIBLE WE OBTAIN
THE BEST POSSIBLE.'

ITALIAN PROVERB

'All

that we do

is done _{with an eye to something else}

with an eye

to something else.'

ARISTOTLE

Other Thorogood titles in this series

The Concise Adair on Leadership
Edited by Neil Thomas
£9.99 Paperback ISBN: 1 85418 218 8

Here in one short book is a practical master class in how to manage both yourself and others, to provide a team that is motivated, creative and high-performing. It encapsulates the essentials of Adair's writing on leadership and effective practice.

The Concise Time Management and Personal Development
By John Adair and Melanie Allen
£9.99 Paperback ISBN: 1 85418 223 4

This is both an expert and practical book to help you manage your time more effectively. It also shows you how to link daily action planning to the achievement of clearly identified long-term goals. It provides the tools, techniques and framework for continuing personal development and will prove invaluable in planning your own self-management as well as your career development.

The Concise Adair on Communication and Presentation Skills
Edited by Neil Thomas
£9.99 Paperback ISBN: 1 85418 228 5

Here in one book is everything you will ever need to know about good communication, presented by an acknowledged expert. This is an excellent introduction for anyone new to the subject and equally valuable as a constant refresher course for the more experienced. It covers: listening, reading skills, speaking and presentation skills, one-to-one interviews and managing meetings.

The Concise Guide to Telephone Tactics
By Graham Roberts-Phelps
£9.99 Paperback ISBN: 1 85418 278 1

Everything you will ever need to know about using the telephone in business by an expert sales trainer. It is divided into three sections: telephone tactics for customer satisfaction, gaining appointments and achieving better sales by telephone.

The Concise Adair on Team Building and Motivation
Edited by Neil Thomas
£9.99 Paperback ISBN: 1 85418 268 4

This book develops Adair's classic theory on Team, Task and Individual and summarises all his writing on leaders and motivation and getting the best from people. It includes sections on being motivated oneself, selecting people, target setting and reward and recognition.

Thorogood has an extensive range of books, professional insight reports and special briefings.

For a full listing of all Thorogood publications, or to order any title, call Thorogood Customer Services on 020 7749 4748 or fax on 020 7729 6110. Alternatively view our website on www.thorogood.ws.

BUSINESS SEMINARS

Focused on developing your potential

Falconbury, the sister company to Thorogood publishing, brings together the leading experts from all areas of management and strategic development to provide you with a comprehensive portfolio of action-centred training and learning.

We understand everything managers and leaders need to be, know and do to succeed in today's commercial environment. Each product addresses a different technical or personal development need that will encourage growth and increase your potential for success.

- Practical public training programmes
- Tailored in-company training
- Coaching
- Mentoring
- Topical business seminars
- Trainer bureau/bank
- Adair Leadership Foundation

The most valuable resource in any organisation is its people; it is essential that you invest in the development of your management and leadership skills to ensure your team fulfil their potential. Investment into both personal and professional development has been proven to provide an outstanding ROI through increased productivity in both you and your team. Ultimately leading to a dramatic impact on the bottom line.

With this in mind Falconbury have developed a comprehensive portfolio of training programmes to enable managers of all levels to develop their skills in leadership, communications, finance, people management, change management and all areas vital to achieving success in today's commercial environment.

WHAT FALCONBURY CAN OFFER YOU?

- Practical applied methodology with a proven results
- Extensive bank of experienced trainers
- Limited attendees to ensure one-to-one guidance
- Up to the minute thinking on management and leadership techniques
- Interactive training
- Balanced mix of theoretical and practical learning
- Learner-centred training
- Excellent cost/quality ratio

FALCONBURY IN-COMPANY TRAINING

Falconbury are aware that a public programme may not be the solution to leadership and management issues arising in your firm. Involving only attendees from your organisation and tailoring the programme to focus on the current challenges you face individually and as a business may be more appropriate. With this in mind we have brought together our most motivated and forward thinking trainers to deliver tailored in-company programmes developed specifically around the needs within your organisation.

All our trainers have a practical commercial background and highly refined people skills. During the course of the programme they act as facilitator, trainer and mentor, adapting their style to ensure that each individual benefits equally from their knowledge to develop new skills.

Falconbury works with each organisation to develop a programme of training that fits your needs.

MENTORING AND COACHING

Developing and achieving your personal objectives in the workplace is becoming increasingly difficult in today's constantly changing environment. Additionally, as a manager or leader, you are responsible for guiding colleagues towards the realisation of their goals. Sometimes it is easy to lose focus on your short and long-term aims.

Falconbury's one-to-one coaching draws out individual potential by raising self-awareness and understanding, facilitating the learning and performance development that creates excellent managers and leaders. It builds renewed self-confidence and a strong sense of 'can-do' competence, contributing significant benefit to the organisation. Enabling you to focus your energy on developing your potential and that of your colleagues.

Mentoring involves formulating winning strategies, setting goals, monitoring achievements and motivating the whole team whilst achieving a much improved work life balance.

For more information contact Kate Jackson on:
+44 (0)20 7729 6677

Falconbury Business Seminars
10-12 Rivington Street, London EC2A 3DU, UK